Bil Keane has been interviewed many times, but here is a first. An [interview] with Jeffy, one of the star performers in "The Family Circus" [cartoon]

Q. Jeffy, will you answer a few questions for me?
A. *(Nodding head.)*

Q. Okay. How old are you?
A. *I'm three fingers old.*

Q. And how old is your daddy?
A. *A hunnert fingers old.*

Q. Do you like the cartoons he draws?
A. *Sometimes. But I ALWAYS like the ones my brother Billy draws.*

Q. Why is that?
A. *The drawing looks better to me.*

Q. Do you ever help your daddy?
A. *(Head nod.)*

Q. In what way?
A. *By staying out of his studio.*

Q. Is he the boss around your home?
A. *No, Mommy is.*

Q. Is your mommy a good cook?
A. *(Head nod.)*

Q. What's your favorite thing that she cooks?
A. *Fritos.*

Q. Fritos? Wait a m[inute...] to cook them.
A. *No. Sometimes we eat them raw.*

Q. Do you like to watch television?
A. *(Head nod.)*

Q. What's your favorite show?
A. *Cartoons.*

Q. Which ones?
A. *The Saturday morning ones.*

Q. How about books? Do you like to read books?
A. *(Head nod.) 'Cept I didn't learn to read yet.*

Q. Of course. You're only three.
A. *But I learned how to look at the pictures. I learned that when I was little. And, know what? I'll be four when my birthday cake comes around again. And Dolly's my sister. She says I'll never get to be as old as she is. But, know what? Grandma says nobody should smoke 'cause they'll get dead and...hear that?...*

Q. Where are you going? Jeffy?...Jeffy, come here...

(Interview concluded because of fire truck going by the house.)

13

15

17

20

21

23

29

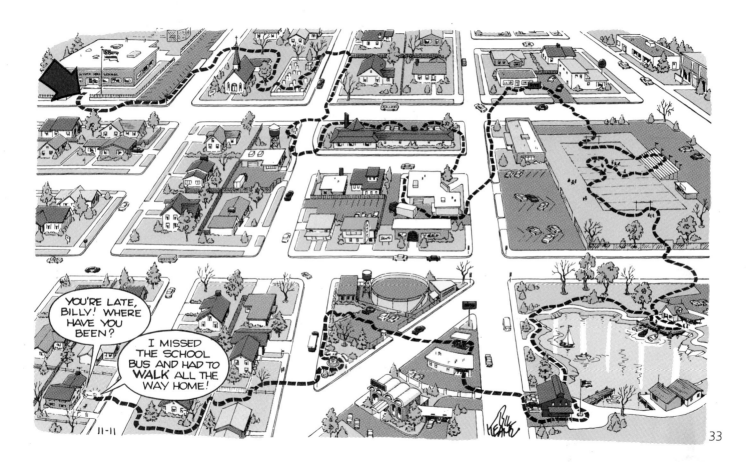

Daddy talking to Grandma on the phone

While Bil Keane takes Father's Day off, 7-year-old Billy draws this family expose.

Jeffy eating all his food

Fried Chicken to go

Mommy getting dinner ready

PJ while Mommy's on the phone

Dolly making toast

Barfu burying his bone

Grandma visiting
our House

Kittycat and her
Scratching post

43

We're goin' over to play in McCauley's pool.

49

53

57

GOODBYE, ALL!

SO LONG!

ADIOS, OL' FRIENDS.

NICE KNOWIN' YOU.

THANK YOU FOR EVERYTHING, MOMMY.

FAREWELL!

SCHOOL

BIL KEANE

65

70

71

79

80

CANCER
THE CRAB

AQUARIUS
THE WATER BEARER

LIBRA
THE BALANCE

PISCES
THE FISHES

ARIES
THE RAM

CAPRICORN
THE GOAT

91

93

Occasionally Billy is pictured taking "the long way around" leaving a graphic dotted line behind to show readers where he has been. Here is a look behind the scenes revealing how that famous dotted line is produced.

STORAGE WELL FOR DOTTED LINE

SHOULDER HARNESS

ON OFF

EXIT SLOT

BATTERIES